DATE DUE

MAR 2 0			
My 18 1992			
APR 1			
APR 20			

Sports World

Swimming

Donna Bailey

Today, I'm going to swim in the big pool for the first time.

My teacher puts some floats on me.
They will help me keep my head out
of the water.

I get in the shallow end of the pool.
The water feels nice and warm.

I bob up and down in the water.
My floats make it easy.

I can put my hands on the bottom
of the pool.
I am learning to swim.

6

This is my swimming class.

We hold on to the rail.

We kick our legs as hard as we can.

I let go, paddle with
my hands, and kick hard.

8

Now I don't need floats anymore.
We see who can splash the most.

We each have a kickboard to help us.
We hold our kickboard and kick our legs.

The harder I kick, the faster
I go through the water.

My teacher shows me how to do the crawl.
She tells me how to move my arms and legs.

Sometimes the water gets up my nose,
but that's okay with me.

I am learning to do the breaststroke, too.
I kick my legs like a frog and
push hard with my hands and arms.

14

I can float on my back.
Next, I will learn the backstroke.

Now we are learning to dive.
We all jump into the water together.

Next, we put our hands
above our heads and dive.
We go headfirst into the water.
When I'm good at swimming and diving,
I want to swim in a race.

These men are in a swimming race.
A good dive gives them a fast start.

18

The first person to touch the bar at
the end of the pool wins the race.

These men are in a backstroke race.
They swim straight down the pool.

These swimmers are making patterns
in the water and with their bodies.

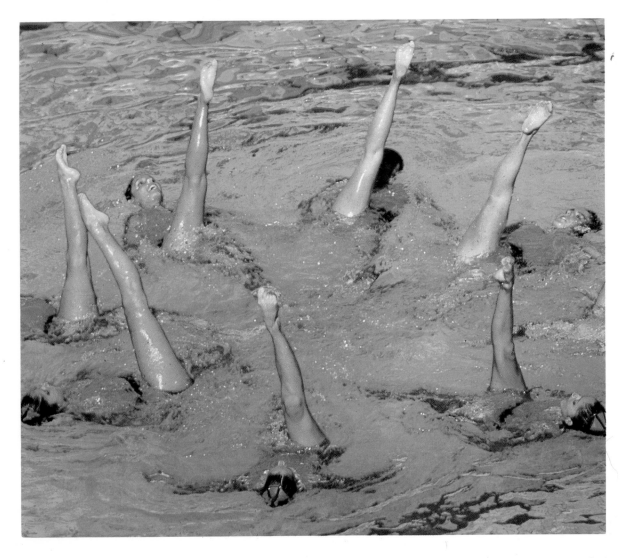

Some swimmers even make patterns when they dive under the water.

This girl is diving off a springboard.
She turns a somersault in the air
before she reaches the water.

Diving like this takes practice.
You must keep your body straight and
your hands in front of you.

Many good swimmers like to snorkel so they can see fish and plants as they swim. They wear a mask, flippers, and a snorkel. A snorkel is a tube for breathing under water.

This girl is scuba diving.
She wears an air tank on her back and
breathes through a tube in her mouth.
She sees many things under water.

Divers can stay under water a long time.
Some divers work on oil rigs.
Other divers explore wrecks on the seafloor.

This ship is the *Mary Rose.*
Divers built a crate around it under water.
Then it was lifted from the seafloor.

Many people like to surf.
They ride surfboards on the big waves
that roll onto the beach.

It takes a lot of practice to
stand up on a surfboard!

Lifeguards watch the people in the water.
They are always ready to rescue someone.

Sometimes they teach classes in lifesaving. Learning about safety and swimming is fun!

Index

Reading Consultant: Diana Bentley
Editorial Consultant: Donna Bailey
Executive Editor: Elizabeth Strauss
Project Editor: Becky Ward

Picture research by Jennifer Garratt
Designed by Richard Garratt Design

Photographs
Cover: Lupe Cunha Photo Library
Allsport: 21,22,23,24
Peter Greenland: title page, 2,3,4,5,6,7,8,9,10,11,12,13,14,15,16,17
Hutchison Library: 32 (Hilly Janes),31
Mary Rose Trust: 28
Tony Stone Worldwide: 19 (Thomas Zimmermann), 26 (Chris Harvey), 27 (Mike Smith), 30 (Paul Berger), 18,20,25,29

Library of Congress Cataloging-in-Publication Data: Bailey, Donna. Swimming / Donna Bailey. p. cm.—
(Sports world) SUMMARY: Shows a girl and her classmates learning to swim and dive. Highlights such aspects
of this recreation as types of strokes, professional competitions, and water sports. ISBN 0-8114-2852-4
1. Swimming—Juvenile literature. [1. Swimming.] I. Title. II. Series: Bailey, Donna. Sports world.
GV837.6.B3   1990   797.2′1—dc20   90-36527   CIP   AC